SANCTUARY: LOVE POEMS

ACKNOWLEDGMENTS

I would like to thank my husband, Rick; our family, friends and colleagues; the poets and writers of Arizona State University, notably Beckian Fritz Goldberg, Alberto Álvaro Ríos, Norman Dubie, Jewell Parker Rhodes and Jeannine Savard; Karla Elling; the late, great Jim Green; Gregory Castle; Michael Vanden Heuvel; Carolyn Forché; Helene Rollins; Meg and Jim Files; and Elena and Jim Thornton. Without their love and support, this chapbook would not be possible.

ISBN No. 978-0-9861200-6-0 "Sanctuary: Love Poems"

SANCTUARY: LOVE POEMS

By Rebecca Dyer

For Rick
Without your love, I am a noisy gong or a clanging symbol

TABLE OF CONTENTS

PART ONE

PART TWO

SANCTUARY: LOVE POEMS

PART ONE

Chiaroscuro

For Beckian and Richard, a Tribute in the Irish vein

Her hair is the black drizzled from his paintbrush,
her eyes the hummingbird outside his window.
He opens their kitchen window on his canvas,
shades a bowl of pears with her cheeks.
Sugar water quivers in the glass feeder.
He dips his brush in thinner,
grains a breadboard with her thighs. A clock chimes,
the hummingbird returns to her nest.
He stretches his back, pulls a straw broom from the corner,
threads it loosely with light.
Sweeps up the warm shadows,
rims with her sighs a cold sink.

Woman on the Cusp

For Ann Bergin

A woman's eyes are the deep, impenetrable green of her jungle,
lined like the sun-cracked shores of her deserts.
Hot winds shift and crumble her breasts' red sands.
Every inch of her resists settlements.

If she is lucky, an attentive lover has only begun to explore her.
He wades to her shore and cakes himself in her mud.
He tracks her spore through the undergrowth,
sleeps fitfully wedged in her branches.
Miles away, at the heart of this young jungle, a girl
opens like a pomegranate.

Stretch of Faith

For MMR

There's never been a man
you didn't want to go
toe-to-toe with.

Like a rock you climb —
intimate with
his faults,
treacherous smooth places.

You've been abandoned
more than once to a narrow ledge, each time
more skilled at letting yourself down.

Sometimes, you are the rock:
Ice cracks in your veins,
your inner stone heaves,
waiting for one man to climb without ropes.

You choose your move —
rather, it chooses you:
a crack to the right, then up.
Thin life line,
enough to wedge yourself in.

Your legs are columns of sand.
Thunderheads hang over you,
a hawk cries in your ear.
You must move, you have no choice.

You pour into your fingers, chalked and sinewy.
A cloud breaks,
splinter of sunlight
strikes your heart like flint.

The Life You Save
When You Suspend Disbelief

What if at the light Janet Leigh (not her real name) had seen her lover (whom no one remembers) cross from her right instead of her boss. If she had thought about striking her horn or for the celluloid tension cranked her window, possibly breaking a nail, nevertheless getting it down and in a very loud stage whisper, "Pssssst, Paul!" — no wait, that wasn't it, it was … it was … S something … Sssssss … Sssssss … Sam! (yes, that was his name!) or louder still "Sam!!!" and if he had heard her or if he hadn't, his eyes focused on the very large breasts of a woman coming toward him, a woman in white, her leash on a greyhound. And if she — the woman crossing — not Janet (nee Jeanette) — if she had made eye contact and if he were licking his upper lip — it was a hot, downtown Phoenix day — and had made some innocuous but not unpleasant remark about her dog. And if she, interpreting his tongue-like gesture as a sign he was thirsty, and well, she was thirsty too, had suggested he buy her something long, tall and wet or maybe just wet and if he had laughed casually, "Guess we should get out of the street." And if she had laughed back, "I know a little place around the corner." And turning together they had seen someone frantic, waving to them from a car, a woman, now slamming her horn, would he then have heard Marion's first whisper, yes, that was it, that was her name. Would he have dropped the walk-on role, strode to her passenger side, a man more of deed than thought, and unashamed of her driving, had gotten in and she, instead of the usual, "Who were you with just now?" instead, more herself, had said, "Oh Sam, Sam, I have thousands of dollars with me, none of it my own —" would he have replied, "Marion, just drive …"

Colorado Trilogy

For my grandparents

What's Expected

After gusts of wind billow white sheets
and Grandma Campbell pinches them down with clothespins
she says to me, Dorothy, now that you're 14
you should know what's expected of a woman.
She should give up any career once she's married.
She should never give a man what he wants but what he needs:
a clean house, respectful children, a hot supper.
She should attend to her fiscal duties — Dorothy, are you listening? —
I said fiscal, not physical.
He earns the money, she pays the bills.
She should give of her affections freely, but only in the bedroom.
She will grow to love him.
I'm left alone to hang the wash. It seems to me the wind
will rip those sheets right from the line.

Promise Me

you won't sneak out to dance.
Your mother did, when we had
the boarding house in Granite.
Flo and Joe, your father, would dance
until 3 in the morning — she a principal
of her own school. Once I told her,
You'll have children of your own someday,
then you'll know what heartache is.
She laughed and kissed my hand.
Now her little John William's gone,
not even a month old.
If you're going to dance, Dorothy,
don't leave by the back door.

Feeling My Way

I'm wearing taffeta
black like a butterfly wing in the dark,
a shimmering salmon red under the chandelier
whose crystals are icicles at dawn.
You, my blind date, your hair slicked back with pomade,
wear your tux like a too-tight second skin.
Your hands abandoned by their sleeves
seek refuge among the table's smoky glasses.
It's a New Year's Eve dinner-dance at the Hotel Denver
and Duke Gillespie, never without a cigarette
hanging from his mouth, introduces us:
This is Dorothy Couse, rhymes with louse.
This is Mark Mills, everybody calls him Mike.
You are a senior at the School of Mines,
I have my own hosiery repair.
Duke, fortified with belts of bathtub gin, roars from his chest.
You laugh with your eyes. Your eyelids disappear
like the roll-top of a desk, seeing fully, loving what you see.
Your nooks and crannies analyze, store away parts of me.
I chatter about winning the department store business,
how they sent their stockings to me when I summered in Cripple Crik.
You listen as though it's the first time you've heard human speech.
Toward midnight you wear your party hat like a rhino's horn,
you make me laugh, push gently into my life.
When we dance, your words crackle with peppermint,
your hands delicate, touching me tentatively, taking samples.
You're not at all like the diamond bit driller from Montana.
Frank Pope, my father called him The Pope, he was Catholic,
loved me with hands like great slabs of ham,
rough because that's all they knew.
When I dance with you, Mark, for I shall call you Mark,
I am in a tunnel sealed off from what was before,
feeling my way ahead in the dark.

PART TWO

The Courtyard

We planted peace roses and sweet peas,
hyacinth and honeysuckle,
tall white walls kept love in.
One day we opened our gate to a wild dog,
believing it could be tamed
merely by being in our presence.
Instead it has destroyed anything with roots,
clawed our bushes,
stripped our flowers,
kept away any visitors.
Curiously, it has not come after us,
but with low prowls and growls
forever traps us in this place of our design,
where once we thought we could live.

Love Notes

For Rick

I'm looking for the soft spot under your wrist
before hair and tendon,
the place worn smooth for sanctuary.

I'm feeling for the rough lines on your knees
where I scrape my hands
climbing to our mountain shelter.

I'm following a stream flowing from your mouth
covered with ferns
I spread to drink.

I've reached the smooth stretch on your thigh,
hitched a ride
on this quiet road.

***

Asleep we move in and out of each other's dreams.
You rise and I fill
the space you've left,
disappear down the back alleys of your bed crease.
You piss lightly, hips swaying like Brahman.
Naked against the ivory backdrop of a night light,
you're a Japanese print from the floating world,
a man washing from a wooden bucket, half-turned,
holding to himself his last vulnerability.
Outside, wind bangs a school crossing sign.
You flick off the light,
cross to the blinds half-open.
Red lights on a plane tail evaporate into darkness.

***

Your pelvis is a delta where the world's rivers end.
In the middle, a shade tree rooted to a sandbar.
I've navigated my own way here,
negotiated rough passages to sleep under your branches.
I was told I would find food,
that your fruit bore knowledge of myself.
I tear a fig from its leaves.
The flesh is soft, yielding against my teeth.

***

Half-asleep, holding your pillow close,
you murmur to be left alone.
Undeterred, I slide into bed,
spoon your body,
kiss your shoulder in a question
and goose chills ripple your skin.
Tiny buds reach for my fingers
as if for light in this dark room.
Even now, in our ninth year,
your body can't resist answering me.

***

On the day of the dead I will not forget you.
I will crawl inside your mouth and start a mambo,
your teeth for my marimba.
My left foot will pound your tongue's bass drum,
my right foot will strum your epiglottis.
Our loved ones, living and dead,
will snake through the room,
twisting to our rhythms. The slow dances
I will dedicate to your memory.

***

I hike the curves of your inner ear,
dynamite the eardrum to reach
your cave of subterranean secrets
stretching for miles in all directions.
I take Polaroids in each chamber,
forever burning a ghastly white image on your pristine walls.
Later, when other scientists conduct their tours,
they will note my crude explorations roped off with velvet cords.
Visitors caught taking artifacts will lose their hands.

***

I am a pilgrim to the wailing wall that is your lower back.
I know it by the twin mounds rising above Jerusalem.
Righteous of all buttocks, these mounds
where I set my tents to lie on your soft brown sands.
I hold my candle close, pray at your wall in a nightlong vigil,
trace the scars carved there.
When the sun rises from behind your head
I will take flight with the twin doves that are your shoulders.

Plantings

You straddle a berm for snap beans, tamp the soil gently
as you would my breasts: Agricultural scientist,
studying the blue vein that crosses my right areola.
Gnats flash in glass bits above water
stagnant in the wall's drainage holes.
Grass is lusher in the shadows there,
a corner of the side yard where no one goes.
I cup a small green tomato, Early Girl,
as I would your testes,
come away with your scent on my fingers.

I remember when you laid the sod in the dark at Easter,
arranging the patches like livingroom carpet
inaugurated with our lovemaking.
But without warning a bog spreads from the far corner,
threatening every growing thing.
Our bougainvillea is drowning, its companion
the Queen Anne's lace clings for life.
Not even their berms can save the peppers
planted for early light.
You say a hardy bush, anything with thorns,
will soak it up, discourage intruders.
But against our best precautions the bog takes possession,
smothering all. Nothing reflects in its ooze.

Over time, cut off from what you love,
your hands begin to wither.
I watch you pale, lie in bed without moving, eyes turned inward.
Soon you leave me.
I weep on our threshold, cursing the bog.
Suddenly it speaks in words I do not understand.
But in its voice I hear crickets and cicadas,
tendrils tentatively curling,
ants dragging twigs to nests,
slight movements that make up a yard.
I see you in a corner planting,
disappearing into a long afternoon shadow.
The bog catches my tears in what must be hands
and as it recedes
grass sprouts from a billion tiny eyes.

Postcards From Florida

I
Low clouds catch us where we stand.
Who knew the roots would hold —
how we're pines clinging to sand.
We tangle the lowest clouds in our branches.
The rest we shatter.

II
Our speedboat tugs at its mooring.
I watch a heron melt into stanchion, reflection
breaking on water. Our skipper
throws off the rope, jumps in beside us,
guns the engines. We're thrown off-balance
as the boat slices water cleanly like a scalpel.
A flying fish just misses our bow.
Soon, we're airborne under our own
blue and white canopy, flung into a conch sky.
I wonder how long we can stay aloft as the wind
jolts our harnesses. Later, breathless on land
we crunch across beach, clouds in our shoes.

III
Heat is an iron pressing against our clothes.
We're earth-bound astronauts boarding the bus,
faces against glass in this artificial cold.
The bus driver with the infinite sang-froid
of a humid afternoon, gestures toward an alligator —
rather, its eyes, a few small bubbles.
An eagle descends into its rooftop nest.
Inside, a shuttle sleeps.
Water tanks are giant mushrooms ready to cool thrusters.
A tortoise hunches across the runway.
Your reflection in the window, I sit back,
daydreaming your beardlike rushes.
I'm floating down your inlet maze.

Also by Rebecca Dyer

"What We've Come Here For"
Poems

Available on Amazon.com

**Praise for poems by Rebecca Dyer:
"What We've Come Here For" ...**

*There is an intricacy in "What We've Come Here For" that makes the journey
through each poem a pleasure. People blend into their physical settings as we
encounter them, but are always highlighted
by a deft sense of observation.*
— **Poet David Chorlton, author of "The Taste of Fog"**

Rebecca's poems enlarge me and comfort me.
— **Poet Frances New, author of "Gift from Maurice"**

Praise for "Sanctuary: Love Poems" ...

In "Sanctuary: Love Poems," Rebecca Dyer finds her inspiration primarily from friends, family, and the worlds in which she lives. The poems in this volume are renderings of lovely human figures interchanging their influences with the natural world, as well as with those of the highly focused witness herself. This poet is unafraid of her vulnerability as she has discovered its ultimate worth in how "A cloud breaks,/splinter of sunlight/strikes your heart like flint." Many of these poems reveal a preservation of beauty, and others, the destruction of what couldn't be maintained, and still more, the recurrent discovery of the need for a necessary yielding for the other's sake, a benefit to all. If you love the sensuous and the reflective, you'll love reading these poems.

— Poet Jeannine Savard, author of "Accounted For"

I remember the sculptor John Waddell lamenting "Do Not Touch" signs, declaring that art, certainly his art, was meant to be touched. Just as pictorial art demands reaction from the eye, so do Rebecca Dyer's poems; but they also demand to be touched. Once touched, they invite the other senses, as well as the Other senses.

— Poet Richard Fenton Sederstrom, author of "Disordinary Light"

Inner and outer experiences flow together in Rebecca Dyer's "Sanctuary," where she achieves a fine balance between the realm of feeling and that of sight and touch. She has created love poems which are firmly located in time and place, in a way that carries them beyond the obvious.

— Poet David Chorlton, author of "The Taste of Fog"

Rebecca Dyer is a poet, journalist and teacher living in Arizona with her husband, Rick. Rebecca and her husband are co-editors of *The Blue Guitar* literary and arts magazine, *The Blue Guitar Jr.* literary and arts magazine for children and teens and *Unstrung* poetry magazine, all non-profit projects of the non-profit Arizona Consortium for the Arts. Contact the poet at RebeccaDyerPoetry@gmail.com.

www.ingramcontent.com/pod-product-compliance
Lightning Source LLC
Chambersburg PA
CBHW020954030426

42339CB00004B/93